A Story of Saint Catherine of Alexandria

A Story of Saint Catherine of Alexandria

By
Brother Flavius, C.S.C.

Pictures by
Carolyn Lee Jagodits

Neumann Press
Charlotte, North Carolina

Nihil Obstat:
    Rev. James O'Halloran, C.S.C.
        Censor Deputatus

Cum Permissu:
    Brother Donatus Schmitz, C.S.C
        Provincial

Imprimatur:
    ✝ Most Rev. Leo A. Pursley, D.D.
        Bishop of Fort Wayne–South Bend

First Printing 1965

A Story of St. Catherine of Alexandria

ISBN: 978-0-911845-03-7

Printed and bound in the United States of America.

Neumann Press
Charlotte, North Carolina
www.NeumannPress.com
2013

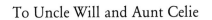
To Uncle Will and Aunt Celie

A STORY OF SAINT CATHERINE
OF ALEXANDRIA

Children are the same the world over. They love to ask questions. They get into trouble. They cause their mothers, their fathers, their aunts and their uncles much concern by their pranks, and then they win their victims over to their side with a beaming smile and a sparkle in their eyes which say, "I love you."

And such a child was little Catherine, a princess of Egypt, the land of the sphinx and pyramids.

"Father, what are stars made of?" asked six-year-old Princess Catherine one day.

"Why, they are specks of light coming from the villas of the gods," he said.

"Why did the gods build their houses way up in the sky?"

"So that they could see you better, Catherine," her father said. "Now run along. It's time for you to go to bed."

Just as King Costus spoke these words to his daughter, her nurse came into the room and motioned to the little girl that her bed was ready. Without any trouble, the little princess kissed her father good night and went off with her nurse to dream like all girls of six.

King Costus was happy the little one was out of his sight for a while. She could ask so many questions!

But his thoughts were broken by his wife, the
Queen Theodora, who came to suggest that he relax
before retiring for the night.

"You have not been outdoors all day," she said.
"Come, let us sit on the terrace."

"I meant to go riding this afternoon," he said,
"but government affairs are so pressing. The
officials in Rome are very demanding and our clerks

must be guided in filling out the forms Rome sends us."

Soon, however, they were on the terrace where they lost themselves in the very serious discussion of their daughter's future.

"It is about time Catherine began formal studies away from the palace, Costus," said his wife.

"I know it will be difficult for me to let her go, but I realize time will not stand still for me. True, I would have Catherine the child stay dependent upon us all her life, but that cannot be," said her husband in agreement.

And, indeed, in no time at all the childish laughter of Princess Catherine was no longer heard about the palace. She had been sent to the school nestling on the mountain near the shores of the Mediterranean Sea. Here she would be instructed with children of other rich families.

Without a doubt, Catherine was a brilliant student. Quick to understand and pleased with all that was taught her, she learned rapidly and eagerly.

Time passed swiftly in school, and Catherine so grew in wisdom and knowledge that her teachers felt that it would be better now for her to return to the palace in Alexandria where she could be taught by the wise men of the city. Other masters, more learned than the ones she had before, were sent for. They came to the palace and instructed her in all the then-known subjects. How happy Catherine was.

Many sands of time passed through the hour-glasses of the royal court, and before Costus and his wife Theodora realized it, their daughter had become a wise and lovely young woman.

Because she was beautiful and kind, many

wealthy men of Alexandria called at the palace to visit her and to ask for her hand in marriage.

Her mother was worried, however. She had just become a Christian, and she did not want her daughter to be given in marriage to a pagan. What could she do? If only Catherine would become a Christian. Catherine had listened to the holy hermit Adrian when he had explained the teachings of

Jesus Christ. It was surprising, indeed, that the brilliant girl did not believe.

Thus it was that one day as Theodora met her daughter in the garden that the conversation turned to religion. "What are you thinking about, Catherine?" her mother asked.

"Oh, the beauty and coolness of the garden, Mother," Catherine said.

"Come, now, a pretty girl like you has more to think about than the weather and the flowers."

"Yes, you are correct, Mother," she said. "I was thinking about some of the young men who have been visiting us. They are indeed fine boys, but I don't care for any of them well enough to marry."

Catherine then made it perfectly clear to her mother that she would marry no man unless that man was very handsome, had much wealth and was as educated as she was and came from a family with a fine past as she did. And since her mind was made up, her mother decided to let God take care of the matter. And this He did, for Catherine was soon to meet that man.

One night Catherine had a dream, a dream that she still remembers in heaven, the dream she will tell you about when you meet her there.

What was that dream? Well, the Queen of Heaven appeared to Catherine and with her were many saints. Our Lady told Catherine that the saints appearing with her were all of noble or of royal blood.

"If you wish, Catherine," said the Blessed Mother, "you may have one of these for your spouse."

But Catherine, being a pagan, rejected them all.

Then the Blessed Mother showed Catherine her Son Jesus.

Now all of us know that Jesus is the most beautiful of men. Jesus is wealthy, for He possesses all things.

Jesus is a nobleman because He belongs to the royal house of David. And He is wise because He is God.

Immediately Princess Catherine's heart was in love with Jesus, and in her dream Catherine told Our Lady that she wanted Jesus for her spouse.

But Catherine was in for a surprise. Jesus would not have her! Remember, Catherine was still a pagan, and for this reason Jesus would have nothing to do with her.

Jesus said to His Mother, "I cannot have Catherine as a bride for she is not beautiful in My eyes. She is not baptized."

With this disappointment the young princess woke at once, and her eyes were filled with tears. Quickly she ran to her mother, told her the dream and asked about its meaning. Of course, her mother thought that it was merely a dream and laughed at it. But as time went on, her mother saw that it had some meaning to it.

"Catherine," her mother said finally, "tomorrow we shall go to see the holy hermit Adrian. Perhaps he can explain your dream to us."

And Adrian, the holy hermit, did explain the dream.

"Jesus Christ," he said, "would like to have

you for His spouse, Lady Catherine, but He
cannot. You still have sin upon your soul. You
must be baptized and become a Christian. Through
the holy sacrament of baptism your soul will be so
wonderful that Jesus will want you with all His
heart."

Princess Catherine was happy when she heard

these words.

"Mother, I am going to learn all I can about Jesus. I want to become more and more like Him," she said.

Every day thereafter Alexandria's young princess went to the cave of the holy hermit to learn more and more about the Divine Nobleman she loved.

How she enjoyed the simple story of the birth of Christ. But the story of His sufferings and death made her young heart sad, indeed.

"I shall never, never sin again," Catherine told the holy hermit, "if that is why Jesus had to suffer."

But the holy hermit made the young princess happy again when he told her that Jesus had founded His church on earth, and that He still lives on earth in His sacraments.

"And it is through this holy church," Adrian

said, "that Jesus wants to be loved, adored, and served."

Catherine learned to love the teachings of Jesus, as time went on, and her love for Him grew very strong.

Finally Catherine was baptized. At last she was beautiful and precious in the eyes of God.

During this time of her growth in the love and knowledge of Christ, Catherine's father had been away at war near the Mediterranean Sea and received a wound from which he never recovered.

Of course, it was hard for Catherine to lose her father, but her new religion showed her how to accept his death. She was resigned to the ways of God during this time of sorrow.

Shortly after the burial of the king, Catherine was proclaimed Queen of Alexandria. Although a ruler, Catherine, like her father, could only reign

as a petty ruler under the protection of the mighty Roman Empire. But how happy the people of Alexandria were to have the charming Catherine for their ruler. Everyone loved her! Remember, Queen Catherine had become a Christian, and because of her Faith she was very kind to the poor.

"The people of my land are worth more than all the gold in the world," Catherine used to say, "because they were purchased and freed with the precious blood of Jesus Christ."

Catherine grew deeply in love with Jesus as the months slipped by, and she wanted very much to see Him once more.

Our Lord, too, was willing to give the young queen her wish. One night when everyone was asleep in the palace, Jesus again came to Catherine in a dream.

The Divine King told Catherine that He was very happy that she had been baptized.

"Now you share in all My merits," Jesus told her, "and because of this you are very pleasing to Me. Come, Catherine, be My bride." Then the Heavenly King placed a beautiful ring upon her finger.

Immediately Catherine awoke. She looked at her finger and actually saw the mark of the wedding ring Jesus had placed there. How happy Catherine was. She was a spouse of Christ at last.

Her mother, too, was overjoyed when Catherine told her what had happened.

"How good God is to choose a member of our family to be His very own," her mother said. "Remember, Catherine, you must always be a good and holy companion to Jesus."

And from that day on Catherine always had Jesus in her thoughts. He was her only joy and Catherine was to bring many souls to Him.

As in many cases, however, sorrow comes before happiness, and this is what happened in Alexandria.

Refugees started to pour into the city all of a sudden, and before long the crowded conditions were called to the attention of the queen. She asked to see some of the refugees, and from these homeless people she learned that the mighty Roman Emperor Maximinus had spread his persecution of Christians

to the nearby village of Aswan. Needless to say, Queen Catherine welcomed all the fleeing Christians and made her ministers find ways to help them.

"Serve the good God well and you will be at peace in Alexandria." This is what the good Queen Catherine told her new subjects. "We shall do all in our power to help you enjoy the good things we have here in our domain."

Every day news of the spreading persecution was brought to Catherine and she grew afraid.

"Suppose the fight against the Christians reaches our city," she said to her advisers.

"If it does," they answered, "many of our people will have much to suffer."

"Worse still," said Catherine, "many might give up God in order to save their lives."

And before long the Roman emperor's persecution did reach Catherine's happy kingdom. Many families began leaving Alexandria, for it was no longer a safe place for Christians. The emperor's soldiers seemed to be everywhere.

Then one day the Emperor Maximinus himself came to Alexandria. He announced that he would hold a trial of all Christians in the city, but he forgot that Queen Catherine was the direct ruler of her people.

Thus it was that on the day of the trial Maximinus seated himself on a throne of gold and silver directly in front of the images of the pagan gods the Christians would be made to adore.

As the name of a Christian was called out, soldiers would push the man or woman before the emperor. At first he was gentle and simply tried to coax the prisoner to give up Christ.

"All you have to do," he softly said, "is to sprinkle a spoonful of this incense over the hot coals before the statues of my gods. It is that simple, and your life will be spared."

Many gave in to the temptation and paid homage to the false gods. But many, too, loudly praised Christ and were marched off to their deaths as they sang songs of joy.

But suddenly, before the trial had long been under way, a clear voice was heard calling the em-

peror by name, and the crowd broke and made way, for they knew none but their queen would dare approach the might of Rome in this way.

"Stop this brutality and sinfulness," she said. And as she reached the seated emperor, she continued to speak. "You have offended the merciful God too much as it is. There are no gods but the one True God. Be sorry for your sins or you will die."

Maximinus was red with anger. But when he saw the beautiful woman before him, he at once thought of a plan to win her over. He invited Catherine to his palace to talk things over, but his carefully planned trap was a failure. She told him that she was a spouse of Jesus Christ, that she would never honor pagan gods.

"I shall never permit my people to sprinkle incense in honor of your gods," she said.

The emperor then ordered Catherine to be thrown into the palace dungeon and to be tortured. Needless to say, Catherine suffered much, but her loyalty to Christ remained firm. Everyone in the prison soon admired the young queen and wanted to know about this Jesus for Whom she was so willing to suffer. Before long, too, many of the emperor's soldiers and even the emperor's wife were won over to Christ.

The emperor could stand this defeat no longer. Catherine was condemned to die on the wheel. Now this machine was so made that two of its wheels turned in one direction while the other remaining wheels turned in the opposite direction. These movements caused the victim tied to the machine to be ground and chewed into a mass of bloody flesh.

When the time came, Catherine walked up bravely to the instrument of torture and willingly allowed herself to be bound to it. And just like Jesus on the cross, she prayed for the soldiers who were ordered to kill her. Before the machine could be started, however, an angel from heaven came down and struck the instrument such a heavy blow that it fell into many pieces.

Still determined to kill Catherine, the emperor then ordered her to be beheaded. The headsman was ready. The ax fell and Catherine's head dropped into a nearby basket, and her soul soared home to Jesus.

Catherine was just a frail young woman, yet she had the courage of a brave knight. Let us follow her example. With the help of God's grace, we, too, can overcome all that is keeping us from loving Jesus more. Ask Saint Catherine for help in your needs, for before she died she said this prayer: "O Jesus, my Divine Lover, I beg of You that whosoever shall praise Your name in my memory, call upon me to obtain Your mercy, ask my aid at the hour of death or in any necessity, may receive a speedy answer to their prayer."